THE SCIENCE OF HAPPINESS

Discovering Joy in Everyday Life

B. VINCENT

QuantumQuill Press

CONTENTS

CHAPTER 1

Introduction

However, in the science of this equation, Klein offers compelling space-age data encrypted in molecular garb. The science of happiness examines the molecular actors and biochemical plotlines that underlie our joy; it explains why a majority of people report being happy, despite the fact that our genome is so similar to that of the chimpanzee, the universal patriarch of human evolution, the ancestor from which we have inherited pretty much every cell in our body. As frightening as it may seem that life should be just a probability game of chemical reactions, the impact on our everyday living could be tremendously liberating. Understanding why certain actions make us happy may not improve our sense of contentment per se, but simply recognizing that our happiness is a natural extension of these actions may loosen our relentless search for happiness.

In this conversation with the German author Stefan Klein, we talk about his best-selling book, The Science of Happiness, and apply some of his recommendations to yoga practice. The book does a masterful job of taking often abstract psychological research and making it accessible to the reader. Klein's basic premise is that the pursuit of happiness is the surest way to misery, and if we want to be happy, we will need to set happiness aside and take other paths that don't directly lead to happiness but ultimately make us happier people. What are these paths?

Living in the now, taking time for oneself, exercise, and sleep, building relationships, smiling and laughing, nurturing inner peace, doing nice things for others. However, these paths are rarely straightforward and can only be discovered by trial and error. The science of the title even seems to abandon the reader with pithy sayings that admonish us not to take life too seriously because nobody gets out alive, and to live each day as if it were our last because one day it will be.

CHAPTER 2

What is happiness?

Despite happiness being a complex emotion that varies greatly from individual to individual, scientists have, over the years, tried to define it. Dr. Martin Seligman is well known in the field of positive psychology—a field that focuses on understanding individual strengths and well-being. Dr. Seligman believes that measuring happiness is like measuring depression. Much can be learned about depression by asking individuals, "What is causing you to feel joy and engage in life every day?" Like Dr. Seligman, I wanted to understand what makes people feel happy, so I decided that the best way to learn about happiness was to learn about what makes a person happy and content.

When people are asked to define happiness, their responses vary greatly. For some, happiness is sipping a Piña Colada on a tropical beach at sunset. For others, it is holding their grandchildren. And for still others, it is winning an Oscar, Nobel Prize, or Grammy. Happiness is a difficult term to define because it encompasses a variety of feelings and emotions such as joy, contentment, and fulfillment.

Neuroscientists agree that, with few exceptions, our brains can change if they are continually engaged in activities that encourage positive brain growth. This change can take as little as five minutes a day. Regularly engaging in positive activities for a period of six weeks ensures that these activities become habits and the changes in the brain become permanent.

Many celebrities who seemed to have it all—money, fame, beauty, talent, and exciting lives—actually struggled with their inner demons. Tai chi, yoga, meditation, and spending time with others enjoying different activities enhance joy. The big idea that I am offering is that you can be happy and healthy by incorporating simple and effective positive habits into your life.

According to folk wisdom, money can't buy happiness. However, neuroscientists are now discovering that this aphorism isn't entirely accurate. In fact, money can buy happiness, but only if you use it to buy the right things. Research in the field of positive psychology has uncovered key contributors to our happiness.

The Science of Happiness: Discovering Joy in Everyday Life

1.1. Importance of happiness in everyday life

Not only science has endeavored to try to find their theories and conclusions about the theme. Many religions emphasize the importance of being happy and indicate ways of life that would lead to happiness. We also have the great treatises on eudaimonia - the ultimate happiness according to the Greek spirit which caused the appearance of ethics and are very important substance produced by human culture. Today there are philosophical movements based massively in the current scientific studies to support their studies about happiness, the positive psychology.

The human being, in his constant search for survival and well-being, has created several different definitions of what it is to be happy. More serious research on the subject only picked up in the 1980s. Since then, a number of books and articles began to be published - from the point of view of philosophy, psychology, physiology, and religion. Of course, people and researchers before the 80s had already devoted themselves to the study of happiness, but the highest number of published researches occurred after the 80s.

1.2. The role of science in understanding happiness

However, few of these articles are actually about happiness - what it is or how we can find it. If you stop to think about it, happiness is not likely to be among the first topics chosen for scientific inquiry. After all, happiness is subjective; it's a feeling. According to the grand traditions of science, our greatest accomplishments are objective, rational, and logical. They offer certainty and generalizable rules. They stand the test of time. They are relevant, except for those rare occasions when the sports section is under review. They define us as human beings. Yet if three days into the conference no one knows a simple formula for happiness, we will begin to slip further and further from our own definition. To the scientific mind, the effort to uncover the elusive secret of happiness is at risk of appearing irrational, emotional, and perhaps even fruitless.

Is happiness possible? For a species endowed with self-awareness, the capacity for reflection, the ability to second-guess itself, and the vital recognition of the impact of each heartbeat, it is a fitting and courageous quest. Open any newspaper today and you will see that science is everywhere. It is relevant to everything from 93 percent of your everyday thoughts to the morning's sports section. In just a few unusual cases, contributors to the sports section have actually been known to think about something other than statistics.

CHAPTER 3

Factors Influencing Happiness

In addition, individuals who are married and engaged in bigger networks are considered to have greater emotional support, and, in turn, have greater psychological and physical well-being. Friendships appear to be equally important predictors of both affective and cognitive well-being. In particular, close relationships tend to have a strong influence on the positive appraisal of life circumstances. In this perspective, the presence of a greater number of friends and relatives who provide help, security, and affection also represents an important element of psychological well-being.

Once basic needs for food, warmth, and pleasure are satisfied, our social environment plays a primary role in our sense of happiness. Individuals who entertain positive and harmonious relations in terms of love, family, friendship, and romantic relationships have higher levels of life satisfaction. The importance of social participation for subjective well-being and life satisfaction has been confirmed also at the cross-national level. This suggests that life satisfaction increases and becomes increasingly less sensitive to other aspects of life, including personal income, as one's degree of social participation increases.

Several important factors are known to drive human happiness. For instance, the perception of good health and financial control is identified as increasing happiness. Correspondingly, the belief that life is out of one's control decreases life satisfaction. In terms of relationships, marriage boosts happiness for a short time, but job satisfaction, social relations, and having many friends are consistently associated with life satisfaction. Thus, money, health, and ties to other people seem to be consistently related to human happiness. In turn, elements like childhood circumstances and the society in which we live contribute to making our lives more or less satisfying.

2.1. Biological factors

The left and right frontal hemispheres of the brain have different neurological activities. Studies indicate that the anterior aspects of the cortex, also known as the prefrontal cortex (PFC), are particularly important for positive emotional response processes, with damage to these areas producing symptoms of apathy, irritability, and depressive mood. Our ability to initiate action is thought to be mediated by circuits running from the PFC to subcortical areas, particularly the amygdala and hypothalamus. The left side of the PFC is critically involved in positive emotional response and is hypofunctioning in studies of depression; decreased metabolism on the left side of the PFC is observed among patients experiencing depression. Recent PET studies have confirmed that a shift toward greater left-sided brain activation is also associated with greater happiness. The shift in brain activation is particularly pronounced within the limbic brain, a region containing the cingulated gyrus and cingulum. The PFC also sends stimulatory tonic cortisol signals to the pituitary gland, the effects of which are principally negative, affecting immune and metabolic processes.

Biological factors. Research in happiness has established a number of biological factors involved in happiness. Biological findings concerning happiness are based on self-reports and measurement of electrical impulses in the brain. When people are asked to reminisce about happy experiences, electrical activity is greater on the left side of the brain, particularly in an area called the frontopolar region. However, when people are asked to reminisce about unhappy experiences, there is greater electrical activity on the right side of the brain, specifically in the left prefrontal cortex. Biological differences between happy and unhappy people are also observed when they are in a pretense state. People who are rated as happy and sociable by their peers show increased activity in the left frontal hemisphere on a task that requires them to wave their hand in a certain way in response to visual cue. Sociable individuals also exhibit a tendency to approach other people on impulse when they are in a happy mood.

2.2. Psychological factors

In continuing with the basic distinction between feeling good and being engaged, we can also look at more detailed psychological factors associated with each concept. For example, findings from an extensive Gallup survey of 24,000 employees in a range of companies showed that the primary factors that differentiate very happy, moderately happy, and very unhappy employees include feelings about the people they work with, the company's mission, and the extent of varying daily tasks. On the pleasure side of the picture, anthropological research has supported the presence of emotional universals in a number of domains, including kin relations, initiatives, and success. Children all over the world smile when happy, and they shake their heads to indicate "no". These customs are not learned, but rather arise from our common human heritage.

Just as there is a physical aspect to being happy, psychological factors also play a role. We need to recognize important psychological factors that can shape and influence happiness. Although the distinction between physical and psychological factors is somewhat arbitrary, it helps us to organize our thinking. Social factors, addressed in the second part of this chapter, will also play important roles in shaping our experiences of both pleasure and passion. This layered approach helps to keep the rich complexities of potential influences in perspective.

2.3. Social factors

I also encourage people to be empathetic, inclusive, and emotionally helpful. These positive behaviors will indirectly promote great outcomes such as leveraging and warm social relationships. Ample evidence suggests that the beneficial effects of strong social relationships on health, well-being, and longevity are stronger than ever now. Given these findings, let us embrace a unifying purpose of capitalizing on the immense power of social connections.

Social support systems may also consist of interactions in public spaces like museums, sporting events, and religious gatherings and may involve contacting community centers or help lines or visiting institutional settings like schools and hospitals. Recent evidence suggests that interacting with people in nature might yield greater joy than more manmade settings. Considering that human socialization is a main drive to lower emotional pain and pressure, I would advise promoting social behavior.

At work, we may foster pleasure to interact with our colleagues and clients by being friendly, smiling, making eye contact, remembering names, and acknowledging ideas. We may deepen our friendships and relationships by practicing honest and supportive communication. It has also been shown that a sense of belonging is important in relationships, since it can help us maintain bonds with others rather than withdrawing from social support. Sometimes, it may be beneficial to build and maintain networks of long-term relationships that can provide meaning, purpose, and encouragement.

Positive relationships are a cornerstone of happiness. As human beings, our work lives, family lives, friendships, and love lives are commonly sources of joy and fulfillment. However, to reap the rewards of such sources of joy, we must be able to effectively communicate, trust, and understand others.

2.4. Environmental factors

The mere presence of other human beings is often enough to improve our outlook: When we think of someone at work or at school, it tends to soften the negative edge of any experiences we may have had that day. Laughter is likely the greatest group effect: Those who laugh more and stay together longer tend to be closer. Finally, specific places can lead us to have fairly clear psychological reactions to them, and thus can act as subtle mood enhancers or depressants. According to some research, for example, being outside is often associated with a heightened sense of well-being; walking around with someone we care for can result in a pleasant, connected feeling (especially if that person happens to be pleasant and connected).

2.4. Environmental factors. A growing body of research is beginning to demonstrate just what a profound impact our surroundings can have on our sense of well-being. So far, evidence has shown that we are generally happier in the company of other people. For example, professors Diener and Biswas-Diener note that married people are demonstrably happier than unmarried ones; people in social clubs, such as book groups, are happier than those who are not. Similarly, a study I conducted several years ago with my dear colleague, Dr. Paul Jose, finds that college-age people who attend religious services (and hence are part of a community) at least once every week are happier and more satisfied with their lives overall than those who do not.

CHAPTER 4

Strategies for Cultivating Happiness

To cultivate pointers, such as focusing on one powerful way to improve your life, by practicing gratitude, personal strengths, and optimism, working and having fun, and decreasing anxiety and bad moods. Past positive emotions also make points more likely. And make positive events better upcoming occurrences. As a result, positive emotional mechanics will be in your life more, which will help you achieve the keys. Practice feeling the positive emotions, deep in your body it will stimulate the endorphins which play a role in overcoming difficulty or stress, and you will start observing the positive in others and the world. Practice directing feelings of compassion at around the world when different from yourself, you start connecting with all life, you generate your compassion, and humans easily presented to humanitarian concerns. The overall effect of the positive thoughts helps to determine exactly what keeps the biology from helping you to connect with other people and over time form happy behavior. Dr. Hanson's 8 Ways to Happiness.

Finding peace with yourself, the world as it is, and the people in your life, which opens you up to seeing the positive in yourself, the world, and the people in it. Your anger, fear, frustration, sadness, and other comparable "normal" feelings destroy the happiness inherent in each moment. If you ruminate on negative outcomes of the past or fears about the future, you can make the poor related feelings and disappointment last a long period influencing what you see and select from the world around you. And you can as well influence and confuse all of the good stuff from your inner thoughts. Looking at the negative actually makes people less happy, and experiencing the passage of time more painfully. This was the aspect of the study, the scientists reported in the Journal of Personality and Social Psychology Study.

According to Dr. Hanson's research, the key strategies for cultivating and protecting happiness include:

3.1. Practicing gratitude

This is the gateway activity for the entire gratitude counting method (GCM) series. When you first wake up in the morning, before getting out of bed, think of one thing you are grateful for in your life. This could be a person, an event, that first cup of morning coffee, anything at all you can sincerely feel a sense of gratitude for. Consider each aspect of the thing and why you are grateful for it, how it makes you happy. When negative or unhappy thoughts arise, remind yourself of the things you are grateful for in life. At first, it may be difficult to find these moments of gratitude; you may feel your reserves are completely empty. However, when you are able to focus and sift through the rubble of a negative outlook, the positive moments will appear. In The Happiness Hypothesis, if 'healthy pleasures are an end in themselves, or activities that are undertaken for their own sake, then gratitude fits the bill'.

Happiness can be a practiced trait. By intentionally participating in activities or behaviors that cultivate joy and gratitude, you are better able to meet your potential for genuine happiness. Choose one of the following activities that most resonates with you, practice it every day for two weeks, and then move onto another activity. Contemplating gratitude can hasten the journey to happiness, which in turn brings joy in everyday life. These various contemplations of gratitude attest to the need to actively and repeatedly focus on the words of gratitude to strengthen and intensify positive emotions.

3.2. Engaging in meaningful activities

Forgetting our own self and reaching out to others reveals great powers to heal the soul. In fact, concentrating solely on the self and constantly looking inward is an excellent way to diminish a person's spirit and soul. Moreover, it is only when you forget your own struggle and divert your attention, when you forget your own problems and instead concern yourself with the welfare of those you love, reach out to help others, and lend a helping hand, that you will find the true purpose in your own life. Happiness is not something passive that comes to you, but you have to actively pursue it. One does not find joy by focusing on what you will receive in life. And we know that true joy lies not in what you get, but in what you give. Happiness comes when you give selflessly.

Happiness is about the meaning and engagement that goes into life. When we see that happiness is not something we get, in fact, we only find true joy by giving our own time, attention, or love to others, it becomes the means to living a life. Practicing gratitude, serving others, reaching out in friendship are powerful ways to connect with others, and these are often the most powerful and lasting sources of our happiness and joy. In fact, we may overendeavor to help others discover joy for themselves by example, encouraging them to engage in acts of kindness and friendship.

3.3. Building positive relationships

Beyond creating close friends, understanding your secrets - what makes you specifically vulnerable - may well promote empathy. Babysep and Coleman at the University of California, Los Angeles, found that disclosing hardships in individual custody trials elicits different reactions among courtroom observers, dying on the measures of body language, including the rise of blinking of the person and more frequent looking from one another of the person. These involuntary reflexes of expressing empathy increased the concept of pain. They were found to be even more substantial when the account of the convicted person emphasized the unique degree of the person's suffering, "I feel deeply lonely," compared to more true expressions of universal pain, "I feel lonely."

Some people become close friends after just an hour. It happened when a team at Stony Brook University sat face-to-face in pairs for 45 minutes, taking turns asking and answering 36 increasingly personal questions. Many of the paired students felt closer by the end of the 45 minutes than other pairs of students. Even more impressive was that six months later, several of the students were so comfortable together (highlighted by their willingness to express their thoughts in front of their newfound pals) and those who grew the closest also spent relatively more time together in the real world. Evolution has fine-tuned humans to fit into a society during which many of us just work together well. Answering questions is only one way to bring people together. Discussing matters and true secrets that are so vulnerable to judgment nudge people closer.

3.4. Taking care of physical and mental well-being

Scholars have also shown that regular exercise is linked to greater mental well-being via increased self-efficacy and a sense of more autonomy, purpose, and control over one's life. Exercise also increases endorphin levels in the brain, which enhances the levels of trust we have with others, making us feel better. This is a perfect opportunity to keep in touch with ourselves and accept that taking care of physical and mental well-being is good for our mind, mood, and body and that there is nothing selfish about it. Staying in touch with our bodies means living in and savoring the present. We should take this opportunity to appreciate the simple things in life, such as the warmth of a cup of coffee, the sound of rain on the window, the feel of a loved one's embrace.

When we asked participants in our studies what helped them maintain a sense of well-being or bounce back from stressful situations, most participants talked about taking care of both their physical and mental health. For many, physical activity played a big role in helping them stay emotionally and physically healthy. Walking, biking, and dancing, among other activities, seemed to help people ward off feelings of loneliness or depression. These results are in line with research showing a strong link between physical exercise and good mental wellness. For example, exercise has been shown to be an effective treatment for depression and acts as a buffer against emotional stress. In a recent study of over 646 permanent residents of Santa Monica, CA, participants who had been more physically active within the past week showed less experience of negative emotions during the week and felt happier overall.

3.5. Finding purpose and meaning in life

A life lived in the service of such self-realization is considered a life that is well-lived. A growing body of research documents a significant connection between eudaimonic living and psychological and physical health benefits across adulthood. But meaning in life is also associated with better physical health, as well as with a lower prevalence of certain mental conditions such as depression and suicidal thoughts. Furthermore, purpose in life has been found to be an important factor in health, quality of life and even longevity. In one study, a sense of purpose decreased the risk of heart attack and stroke in a sample of 1367 Finnish participants as compared to people without a sense of purpose. Not only were those with the highest sense of purpose more likely to be alive than those with the lowest purpose, they were significantly less likely to have died from heart disease or sudden death, as well as having a risk of between stroke and cerebral infarct. Previous research had found that this factor is associated with lower scores of depression and with optimism, both of which are associated with physical health because they can generate positive health practices such as regular physical exercise and nutritious meals, and minimize threshold behaviors such as smoking and problem drinking.

Eudaimonic well-being consists of self-realization, obtaining an optimal match between one's most authentic self and the life one leads. This is quite different from subjective well-being, which refers to a more fleeting hedonic aspect of happiness. In other words, it is the positive emotion that is the result of a life well lived. There are different levels of well-being and meaning: an individual may experience feelings of happiness based on momentary well-being without life satisfaction. Someone may feel they have a meaningful life when they report that their daily experiences are characterized by meaning. Thus, meaningfulness is an ongoing construct and it derives from the degree to which people feel their lives have meaning.

CHAPTER 5

Applying Happiness in Everyday Life

The art of happiness can seem stagnant at the level of scientists and not make enough of a leap into the seemingly complicated world of human nature. The way that many cultures absorb this knowledge and knowledge of other research fields is through the media: newspapers, magazines, and various other news outlets. If a study on happiness is reported in the media, it is generally featured as a small piece of health news buried between celebrity gossip and health findings. Rather than pit these trends against each other, NPR launched a program called "Take A Number" that brings numbers into the real world. Take A Number is based on the happiness findings of Adrian White, who researched happiness in different countries and created a world happiness map from it. This map stirred up much excitement and discussion and was even referred to by British Prime Minister Tony Blair. More recently, a poll in the United Kingdom shows what Britons think of this world happiness map.

In today's society, a "self-improvement" mindset is often encouraged, but ways of doing this are rarely provided. Richard Layard, a professor of economics at the London School of Economics, points out that constantly comparing our fortunes to others is not a solution to being happy, but rather to being miserable. Psychotherapist Andrew

Weil, M.D., states that having too much emphasis on the self or self-importance can bring about a sensitivity to slights, which can lead to prolonged sadness. Happy people share a few important qualities, and one includes a healthy perspective on life and relationships with others.

4.1. Enhancing happiness at work

Another important factor that stands out in the work context is the working conditions. In order for employees' needs in their professional lives to be met, it is of the utmost importance that employees have some autonomy. Autonomous work means that employees are less subject to external pressures. Autonomous work is related to positive outcomes such as higher quality work, better mental health, and higher happiness. The needs associated with the role of the manager are the application of the autonomy-supportive leadership style, which is seen as the support provided by managers in meeting the needs of employees by providing them with choices, listening and being understanding, and involving them in decision-making. In organizational research, studies have been conducted on customer satisfaction, employee happiness related to employee retention, reliability, and loyalty. Employees are the visible aspects representing the success or failure of the organization at every stage experienced in the social life perception of the organization.

In order for teams and employees to be successful at work, employee performance should be managed not only by focusing on negative experiences but also by enhancing employee strengths and opportunities to develop themselves, thus increasing happiness. Instead of focusing solely on improving weaknesses, performance management should also focus on employee strengths. The point to be focused on here is shared benefits. In order for employee performance to be managed with this method, managers should be able to carry out evaluations impartially and understand their own biases. Managers are more likely to accurately evaluate their employees' digital selves when their own external feedback is incorporated into the feedback system as well. In this way, managers can manage employee performance by focusing on happiness by using an objective look at their own evaluation.

4.2. Nurturing happiness in relationships

Happiness is an inside job and is not about feeling good all the time. It is not about things always working out the way we want, it is not an expectation that we can, or will ever be able to control life experiences and avoid all of our pains and disappointments. For me, this new understanding about happiness has been a life-changing perspective. Our strongest human longings are to love and be loved, to give and to receive care, to be valued and appreciated, to be a part of intimate loves and authentic relationships. These deep desires are the needs that must be acknowledged, honored, and nourished. These are the things that will ultimately provide us with the happiness in life that we have desired and imagined. There will probably never be a time in which we decide that we are now, and forever, perfectly happy. There will always be some more happiness in shared experiences that we can never see or predict. Uplifted and safe together, we remember and learn to have the joy we have found helping us to cope with the unexpected, the stress and the demands of our ever-changing lives.

4.2. Nurture happiness in relationships. Nurturing real connections, especially with those we value most, can exponentially grow our experience of happiness. How often do you express your thankfulness for the people in your life who mean the most to you? Taking steps to increase the number or quality of intimate relationships that mean the most to us is in our own best interest, because in the end, those care relationships are the most important parts of our lives contributing most to our happiness and life satisfaction. As we look back on our lives, it will be the quality of those family and friend connections that will be important. Furthermore, those care relationships will usually be the source of the most consistent and long-lasting experiences of the positive emotions that give us joy and happiness.

4.3. Incorporating happiness in daily routines

The afternoon drowsiness loop can actually tell time and evade, and eating also helps people manage integrity and prevent drowsiness. From a personal perspective, life satisfaction, pleasurable activity, optimism about the future, social relations, and financial satisfaction increase as people celebrate their day at work (e.g., away from home). Self-growth and built-in indicators show similar growth. For collecting supplies to be metabolized into low levels of physical pleasure and happiness, the average interval between 2 hours of physical activity is 5-15 minutes, and 1-60 minutes. After all, it takes 20 minutes to provide the best cortex; if they can hear the regular sound of the column, such as toiletries, discussions, and the social inequalities. Without continuity, this mark may continue to grow further and cause fatigue, leading to a growing community.

Lunch routines may have a secret power to increase happiness. Whether we carry out the same old dull routine of making breakfast, going to work for hours on end, and then going home after work, or do something different such as going for a mid-morning snack, having a meal in a new restaurant, doing some light exercise, doing something different than before because the day was well-scheduled, and so on, can, in the end, change people's impression of the end of routine, as well as the assessment of the quality of those activities in the long term. Many small changes together can create variety and thus the ability to repeatedly improve happiness over time. Remember Richardson's words – even the smallest change can have the greatest impact.